Life As ...

Life As a Child Laborer During the Industrial Revolution

Andrew Coddington

Cavendish Square
New York

Published in 2017 by Cavendish Square Publishing, LLC
243 5th Avenue, Suite 136, New York, NY 10016

First Edition

Website: cavendishsq.com

CPSIA Compliance Information: Batch #CS16CSQ

All websites were available and accurate when this book was sent to press.

Library of Congress Cataloging-in-Publication Data

Names: Coddington, Andrew.
Title: Life as a child laborer during the Industrial Revolution / Andrew Coddington.
Description: New York : Cavendish Square Publishing, 2017. | Series: Life as... | Includes bibliographical references and index. | Description based on print version record and CIP data provided by publisher; resource not viewed.
Identifiers: LCCN 2016000340 (print) | LCCN 2015048868 (ebook) | ISBN 9781502617736 (ebook) | ISBN 9781502617958 (paperback) | ISBN 9781502617859 (library bound) | ISBN 9781502617651 (6 pack)
Subjects: LCSH: Child labor—History—Juvenile literature. | Children—Social conditions—Juvenile literature. | Children—Economic conditions—Juvenile literature. | Industrial revolution—Juvenile literature.
Classification: LCC HD6231 (print) | LCC HD6231 .C59 2017 (ebook) | DDC 331.3/1—dc23
LC record available at http://lccn.loc.gov/2016000340

Editorial Director: David McNamara
Editor: Kristen Susienka
Copy Editor: Rebecca Rohan
Art Director: Jeffrey Talbot
Designer: Alan Sliwinski
Senior Production Manager: Jennifer Ryder-Talbot
Photo Research: J8 Media

The photographs in this book are used by permission and through the courtesy of: Lewis Wickes Hine/Everett Historical/Shutterstock.com, cover and 20; English Heritage/Heritage Images/Getty Images, 5; Kean Collection/Getty Images, 6; Popperfoto/Getty Images, 8; Universal History Archive/UIG/Bridgeman Images, 10; Time Life Pictures/Mansell/The LIFE Picture Collection/Getty Images, 13; Mary Evans Picture Library/Imagno, 14; Lewis W. Hine/Buyenlarge/Getty Images, 16; Jacob A. Riis/Museum of the City of New York/Getty Images, 19; Mary Evans/M.C.Esteban/Iberfoto, 22; Keystone/Getty Images, 23; PhotoQuest/Getty Images, 24; Belal Hossain Rana/Pacific Press/LightRocket via Getty Images, 27.

Printed in the United States of America

Contents

Introduction

You wake up most mornings and go to school. You might not always like it, but you go and you learn. This was not always the case. At one point in history, many children did not go to school. You may think that sounds great, but imagine if you had to work instead. Many children had jobs in factories doing difficult and dangerous work instead of going to school.

This time in history was called the **Industrial Revolution**. Back then, machines were becoming popular ways to do jobs like make clothes. Adults and children worked the machines. This work was difficult and dangerous. People could lose their fingers or arms or legs, or even die.

During the Industrial Revolution, businesses hired laborers to work machines.

Businesses built huge factories
to house their machines.

Chapter 1

Man and Machine

The Industrial Revolution started in England around 1760. Eventually, it arrived in the United States and lasted until the 1930s. During this time, many new machines were invented. They could make different items, such as clothes, chemicals, glass, and paper.

Machines were very popular with people who owned businesses. They wanted to earn lots of money from the items made by machines. In the Industrial Revolution, machines could make more and better **goods** in less time than one person. Machine-made items could be sold at lower prices, too.

Business owners started opening factories in large cities. Some cities that had many factories were

Children were able to change small parts on machines in tight places.

London, New York City, Boston, and Chicago. To help work the factory's machines, business owners needed many people. They posted advertisements for workers. People started moving from their homes in the countryside to big cities.

Almost everyone in a family worked. They needed to work to survive. Many fathers, mothers, teenagers, and children all worked in factories. These people were called **laborers**.

Business and Buyers

In order for businesspeople to make more money, they had to sell more things. This led to what is called **consumerism**. People who buy things are called consumers. People had to buy more in order for businesses to make money. For example, in the past, clothes made by hand were expensive. A person may have owned one or two outfits. When machines started making more, cheaper clothing, people could buy many more outfits for the same price.

This boy carries a heavy load of cans.

Chapter 2

Looking for Workers

In cities, families struggled to survive. They could not buy food, clothing, or shelter. Many families expected their children to help support the family by working. Sometimes, families worked together. Other times, everyone worked at different factories or businesses. Many children worked in factories.

Business owners wanted to hire the cheapest laborers they could find. The more money they could save paying workers, the more money they could make for themselves. Businesses did not pay people a fair **wage**.

Business owners liked having children work in their factories. Children could work for a small amount of money. At work, children could fit into spaces adults couldn't, such as in between machines. This meant children could help fix any broken machines. They would work for long hours each day. Some children

Writing About the Industrial Revolution

Charles Dickens was an author from England. He lived during the Industrial Revolution. Many of his books took place during that time and had orphaned children as main characters.

One book Charles Dickens wrote was *Oliver Twist*. This was the story of an orphan who worked in a **workhouse**. Oliver Twist had a hard life in the workhouse and chose to run away rather than work. He joined a gang and lived on the street. The book showed readers how difficult it was for child laborers to find a better life.

worked ten to fifteen hours every day.

Some children did not have to be paid at all. These child laborers were orphans. They lived in workhouses. These factories said the work the children did paid for the costs of housing them.

In *Oliver Twist*, Oliver starts off living in a workhouse.

How Many Child Laborers?

In 1900, about 1.75 million child laborers worked in the United States. They were between the ages of ten and fifteen. Many child laborers were younger than ten.

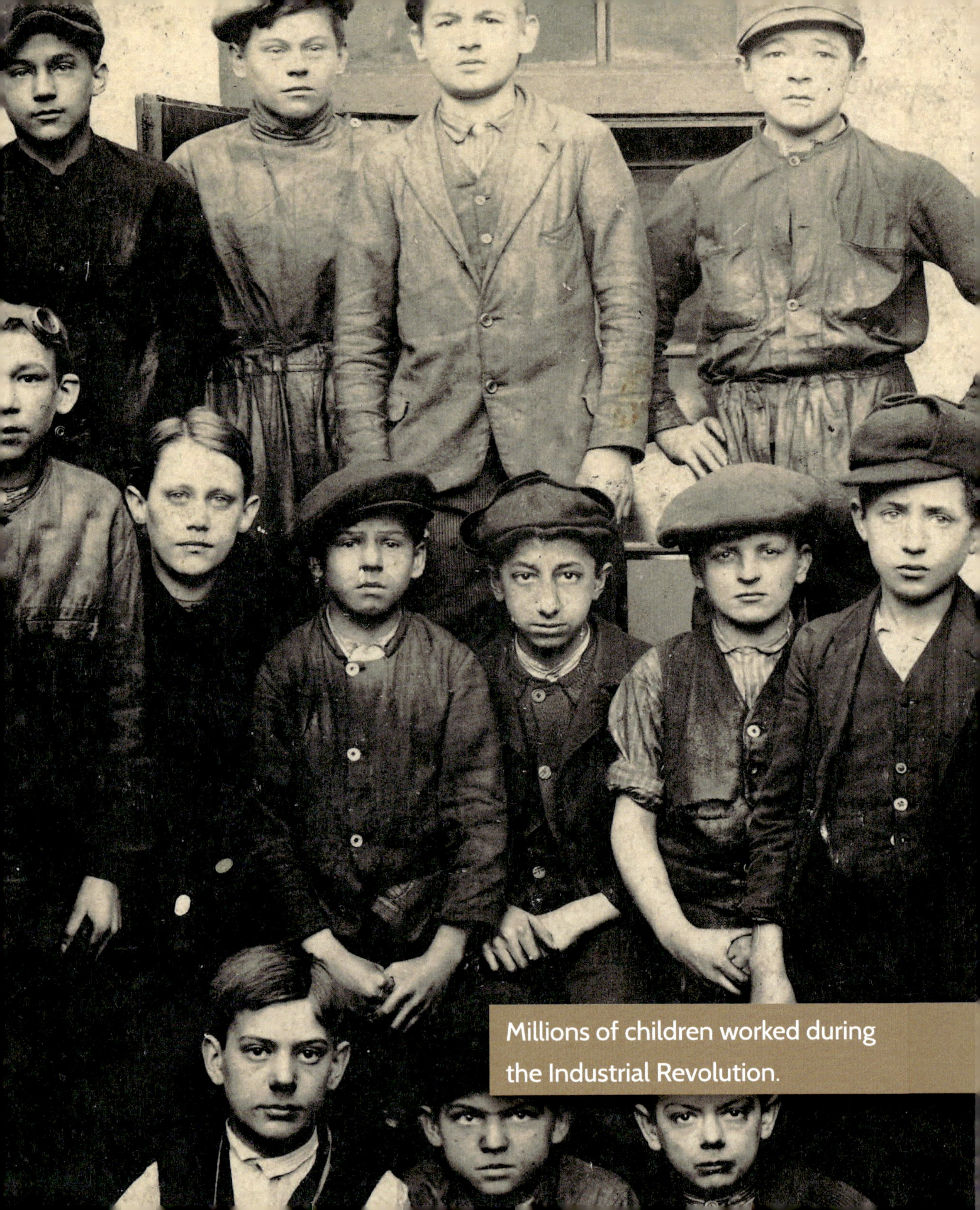

Millions of children worked during the Industrial Revolution.

Chapter 3

Children on the Job

Because children were young, they could be paid a small amount of money. They earned a lot less money than adults. Some child laborers only made about 20 percent, or one-fifth, of what adults made.

Working in a factory was dirty, dangerous, and even deadly. Most business owners did not care about their employees' safety. There were no government agencies to protect people. As a result, many people were seriously injured or even died while at work.

Many children worked in coal mines. Coal was used in the Industrial Revolution to power steam engines. Like a charcoal grill, coal produces a lot of heat when it is set on fire. Heat from coal was

A Day at the Coal Mine

A child who worked in a coal mine might have a schedule like this:

4 a.m.	Wake up and walk to the mine
5 a.m.	Start working
6 a.m.	Separate coal from rocks on a conveyor belt
12 p.m.	Eat quick lunch of porridge, fruit, or gruel
12:30 p.m.	Start working again
1 p.m.	Drag wooden tubs filled with coal through the mines
5 p.m.	End shift and walk home
6 p.m.	Eat dinner with family
8 p.m.	Bedtime before tomorrow's shift

Shoveling coal was just one of the dirty jobs at a mine.

used to turn water into steam, which powered many machines. Children carried coal along narrow mineshafts to the surface. Many children were killed when mines collapsed. Others were crushed to death by heavy carts full of coal. Mines also sometimes exploded when dangerous gases caught fire.

Dangerous chemicals were often used in factories, such as match and glass factories. Children who worked around these chemicals might be burned, blinded, or develop diseases.

Factory bosses had permission to discipline their child laborers. Some child laborers tried to run away from their jobs. When they got caught, their bosses might whip them. Other times, they may be chained to their workstations to keep them from running away again.

Coming home after a long day was not much better. So many people moved into the cities in such a short time that the cities became crowded and dirty. People had to live close to their factories in small apartments called **tenements**. Sometimes multiple families lived in tenements that were only as large as a couple of rooms.

Neighborhoods in cities were also dirty. Many families did not have running water or working toilets. Families simply dumped their filth into the streets. This caused many people to get sick.

Tenements during the Industrial Revolution were dirty, dangerous, and crowded.

This little girl is working at a cotton mill.

Chapter 4

Blood, Sweat, and Tears

Children worked in many different places during the Industrial Revolution. Some children were hired to work in textile mills. Textile machines wove cotton threads into fabric for clothing. Some child laborers in these mills worked on a machine called a power loom. The power loom spun yarn into fabric very quickly. Children working on power looms had to make sure that the fabric was smooth and that parts of the machine did not get stuck. They used their bare hands to feel the fabric and fix the machines.

Textile mills were dangerous places. Children who worked on the machines did not wear gloves to protect their hands. Sometimes, the fabric would

Some child laborers had to drag heavy buckets of coal through dark and cramped mines.

pinch their fingers as it was being spun. Other times, they might lose a finger or even a whole hand if it got caught while they were fixing the machines. Girls who worked in textile mills had to keep their hair short and pulled back. Otherwise, their hair might get caught in the fabric or in the machines.

Other children worked in coal mines. Some children sorted coal on a fast conveyor belt. Many lost fingers and hands. The conveyor belt was powered by a big wheel. Some children fell into the wheel and were crushed.

Child laborers pulled tubs of coal through mines. These tubs were usually made from wood and had curved sides, which made them easier to move along the ground. Coal tubs were usually tied to a belt wrapped around a child's waist. Because mineshafts were very small, workers could not stand up. Children had to crawl on their hands and knees.

Danger in the Dark

Another tool used in coal mines was a headlamp. The light bulb was not invented yet, so people often tied burning candles to their foreheads in order to see in the dark mines. These headlamps were very dangerous. Many mines were filled with dangerous gases. When these gases caught fire, they would explode, burning the miner or destroying the whole mine.

These women are protesting the practice of child labor in the 1900s.

Chapter 5

Fighting to End Child Labor

Near the end of the Industrial Revolution, people started to change their thoughts about children going to work. It became clear that the work children were doing was dangerous and did not give them time to go to school or have fun. Also, adults wanted to do the jobs children did if factories could pay adults more.

Groups known as **unions** worked to protect laborers. Many unions started asking governments to end child labor and to make more jobs for adults.

Child labor in the United States did not end until the 1930s. This happened during the Great Depression, when many companies went out of business. During this time, many adults lost their jobs.

Businesses wanted to hire children because they were cheaper. Unions worked hard to make businesses hire adults. In 1938, the US government passed a law called the Fair Labor Standards Act. Part of that law made it illegal for children under the age of fourteen to work. Instead, children could go to school and have a life outside of work.

Even though child labor does not exist in the United States, it continues in other parts of the world. Children growing up in poorer countries must often work to help support their families. Charity groups are still trying to end child labor around the world.

If you live in the United States or another country that does not have child labor, the next time you do not want to go to school, remember: you could spend all day pulling buckets of coal or fixing machines.

This boy worker is from Bangladesh, where child labor is still practiced.

Glossary

consumerism When customers (consumers) need to buy more in order for businesses to make money.

goods Items made to be sold.

Industrial Revolution A period in history where machines started to replace people making things by hand.

laborer Someone who works.

tenement An overcrowded and rundown apartment that housed multiple families at a time.

union A group of workers that join together to stand up for their rights.

wage An amount of money people are paid for their work.

workhouse A place that took in orphans who were required to work for their food and shelter.

Find Out More

Books

Mullenbach, Cheryl. *The Industrial Revolution for Kids: The People and Technology That Changed the World.* Chicago: Chicago Review Press, 2014.

Otfinoski, Steven. *The Child Labor Reform Movement: An Interactive History Adventure.* North Mankato, MN: Capstone Press, 2013.

Website

Child Labor Public Education Project

www.continuetolearn.uiowa.edu/laborctr/child_labor/about/us_history.html

Video

Child Labor and the Textile Mills

www.gpb.org/georgiastories/videos/child_labor_and_the_textile_mills

Index

Page numbers in **boldface** are illustrations. Entries in **boldface** are glossary terms.

About the Author

Andrew Coddington has written several books for Cavendish Square. He lives in Lancaster, a town in Western New York, with his fiancée and dog.